Tempting CAKES & BAKES

D0508384

*In a world where so much is prepackaged, it is comforting to know
that homemade cakes, biscuits and breads continue to be enjoyed
wherever there are enthusiastic cooks.*

*This collection ranges from simple wholemeal parathas to elaborate
creamy confections which double as desserts. Traybakes, chosen for
their ease of cutting and portability in lunchboxes and picnic baskets,
are included, as are wholesome fruit cakes and loaves suitable
for Sunday afternoon tea. Finally, there's a more than generous dip
into the biscuit barrel, with a selection of sweet and savoury treats.
Many of the bakes are suitable for last-minute cooking. Loaves and cakes
can be frozen, preferably before being iced, then thawed and decorated
when required. To really impress unexpected visitors, keep a few rolls
of biscuit dough in the freezer, ready for slicing and baking while
the kettle is coming to the boil and the tea tray is being laid.
Baking is a highly satisfying form of cookery; the results are certain
to find favour, and you have the added satisfaction of knowing precisely
what went into the biscuits and bakes your family and friends are
devouring so enthusiastically!*

CONTENTS

SWEET SQUARES AND SLICES

Cook a couple of fruit loaves or traybakes this weekend. Easy to cut and convenient for wrapping, they are the perfect choice for packed lunches and picnics.

Banana Loaf with Maple Icing

125g (4oz) butter or margarine

185g (6oz) caster sugar

1/2 tspn vanilla essence

3 ripe bananas, roughly mashed

250g (8oz) self-raising flour, sifted

2 eggs

125ml (4fl oz) natural low-fat yogurt

sliced banana to decorate, optional

Icing

45g (1¹/₂oz) butter or margarine

110g (3¹/₂oz) icing sugar, sifted

2 tspn maple syrup

1 Preheat oven to 180°C (350°F/ Gas 4). Line and grease a 23 x 13cm (9 x 5in) loaf tin. In a large mixing bowl, beat the butter or margarine until soft. Add the sugar, vanilla essence and bananas and continue beating until the mixture is light and fluffy. Add 2 tablespoons of the flour; beat until well combined. Add the eggs, one at a time, beating well after each addition. If the mixture shows any signs of curdling, add a little more of the flour.

2 Gently fold the remaining flour into the creamed mixture, alternately with the yogurt. Spoon the mixture into the prepared tin and level the top.

3 Bake for 1 hour or until golden brown and firm. Cool in tin for 5 minutes, then turn loaf out onto a wire rack and allow to cool completely.

Almond and Apricot Loaf

4 To make the icing, beat the butter or margarine in a small bowl until soft and creamy, then add the icing sugar and maple syrup and beat until smooth. Spread over the cooled loaf. Decorate with fresh sliced banana if serving at once.

Makes 1 loaf

Almond and Apricot Loaf

110g (3¹/₂oz) dried apricots, chopped

60g (2oz) butter

185g (6oz) sugar

250ml (8fl oz) boiling water

1 egg, lightly beaten

125g (4oz) plain flour, sifted

125g (4oz) wholemeal plain flour

1 tspn bicarbonate of soda

60g (2oz) almonds, chopped

1 Preheat oven to 180°C (350°F/ Gas 4). Line and grease a 23 x 13cm (9 x 5in) loaf tin. Combine the apricots, butter, sugar and boiling water in a large bowl. Stir until the butter has melted; cool to room temperature.

2 Stir in the egg, then gradually stir in the flours and bicarbonate of soda mixture. Add the almonds.

3 Spoon the mixture into the prepared tin and level the top. Bake for 1 hour or until golden brown and cooked through. Cool on a wire rack.

Makes 1 loaf

Pumpkin Nut Bars

185g (6oz) butter or margarine
250g (8oz) caster sugar
185g (6oz) plain flour
1 tspn bicarbonate of soda
1/2 tspn baking powder
1/2 tspn salt
1 tspn ground cinnamon
1/2 tspn ground allspice
2 eggs, lightly beaten
60g (2oz) walnuts or pecan nuts, chopped
1/2 tspn vanilla essence
90g (3oz) sultanas
1 x 375g (12oz) can crushed pineapple, drained
125g (4oz) canned pumpkin

Icing

220g (7oz) icing sugar, sifted
90g (3oz) cream cheese, softened
1/2 tspn vanilla essence
2 tspn lemon juice

1 Preheat oven to 180°C (350°F/ Gas 4). Line and grease a 28 x 18cm (11 x 7in) baking tin. Cream the butter or margarine with the sugar in a large mixing bowl until light and fluffy.

2 Sift all the dry ingredients together; add to the creamed mixture alternately with the beaten eggs. Stir in the nuts, vanilla essence, sultanas, pineapple and pumpkin. Mix well.

3 Spoon the mixture into the prepared tin and level the top. Bake for 1 hour or until a skewer inserted in the centre of the cake comes out clean. Cool on a wire rack.

4 Make the icing by mixing all the ingredients together in a bowl. Stir until combined, then beat until light and fluffy. Spread the icing on the cooled cake. When set, cut into bars.

Makes 22 bars

Carrot and Banana Loaf

125g (4oz) butter or margarine
125g (4oz) soft brown sugar
1 egg, beaten
185g (6oz) carrot, grated
2 ripe bananas, mashed
185g (6oz) plain flour
1 tspn bicarbonate of soda
1/2 tspn ground cinnamon
30g (1oz) walnuts, chopped
45g (1 1/2oz) sultanas

1 Preheat oven to 180°C (350°F/ Gas 4). Cream butter or margarine and sugar. Add egg and beat well. Stir in carrot and bananas.

2 Sift dry ingredients together. Add to mixture with walnuts and sultanas. Mix well.

3 Spoon mixture into a greased and lined 23 x 13cm (9 x 5in) loaf. Bake for 1 hour or until cooked when tested with a skewer. Cool loaf in tin for 5 minutes. Turn onto a wire rack to cool completely.

Makes 1 loaf

No Bake Chocolate Log

185g (6oz) butter, softened
4 tblspn caster sugar
4 tblspn cocoa powder
2 egg yolks
15 plain biscuits, crumbled

1 Place butter and sugar in a mixing bowl and beat until light and fluffy. Stir in cocoa, egg yolks and crumbled biscuits.

2 Brush a length of foil lightly with oil. Using a spatula, scrape biscuit mixture onto foil, spreading it out to form a rough log shape. Roll foil over top and mould to a even log.

3 Refrigerate for 2 hours or until firm. Cut into 5mm (1/4in) slices.

Makes about 20 slices

No Bake Chocolate Log

4

Coconut Lemon Wedges

Coconut Lemon Wedges

30g (1oz) coconut macaroons, crushed

60ml (2fl oz) Cointreau

200g (6½oz) desiccated coconut

90g (3oz) butter, softened

2 tspn grated lemon rind

125g (4oz) caster sugar

2 eggs, lightly beaten

2 tblspn lemon juice

1 Preheat oven to 150°C (300°F/ Gas 2). Line and grease a 23cm (9in) springform tin. Place macaroons, Cointreau and 75g (2½oz) coconut in a bowl. Mix. Press evenly into prepared tin.

2 Cream butter, lemon rind and sugar. Beat in eggs, one at a time. (The mixture may curdle; this is not a problem.) Stir in lemon juice and remaining coconut; spread mixture over base.

3 Bake for 40 minutes or until golden brown. Cool in tin. Remove sides of tin. Cut into wedges.
Makes about 15 wedges

Light Chocolate Loaf

220g (7oz) plain flour, sifted

1 tblspn baking powder

1 tspn salt

60g (2oz) cocoa powder

315g (10oz) sugar

250ml (8fl oz) skimmed milk

125ml (4fl oz) sunflower oil

1 tspn vanilla essence

4 egg whites

1 Preheat oven to 180°C (350°F/ Gas 4). Line and grease a 23 x 13cm (9 x 5in) loaf tin. Sift flour, baking powder, salt and cocoa into a bowl. Stir in 250g (8oz) of sugar. Add milk, oil and vanilla essence. Beat until well mixed.

2 In a second bowl, beat egg whites until soft peaks form. Gradually add remaining sugar, beating until stiff peaks form.

3 Fold egg whites into cake mixture. Bake for about 40 minutes or until cooked when tested with a skewer.

4 Cool in tin for 5 minutes. Turn onto a wire rack to cool completely.
Makes 1 loaf

Wholemeal Apricot and Coconut Loaf

90g (3oz) desiccated coconut
185g (6oz) dried apricots, chopped
250ml (8fl oz) hot milk
60ml (2fl oz) clear honey
1 egg, lightly beaten
90g (3oz) wholemeal flour
30g (1oz) ground almonds
1 tspn baking powder
2 tblspn lemon juice
2 tblspn sugar

1 Spread out coconut on a baking sheet; toast it under a hot grill or in a moderate oven for 5 minutes or until golden. In a large bowl combine apricots, milk and honey. Cover and set aside for 1 hour.

2 Stir egg, flour and almonds into apricot mixture. Mix well. Stir three-quarters of the toasted coconut into cake mixture; reserve the rest for topping.

3 Preheat oven to 180°C (350°F/ Gas 4). Line and grease a 23 x 13cm (9 x 5in) loaf tin. Spoon cake mixture into prepared tin and level top. Bake for 45 minutes or until a skewer inserted in centre of loaf comes out clean. Cool cake in tin for 5 minutes.

4 Meanwhile heat lemon juice and sugar in a small saucepan until sugar has dissolved. Remove cake from tin. Brush top with lemon mixture while still warm; sprinkle with reserved toasted coconut.

Makes 1 loaf

Date and Yogurt Squares

90g (3oz) butter or margarine
125g (4oz) caster sugar
grated rind of 1 lemon
2 eggs, separated
125g (4oz) self-raising flour, sifted
1/2 tspn mixed spice
150ml (5fl oz) plain yogurt
125g (4oz) pitted dates, finely chopped

1 Preheat oven to 180°C (350°F/ Gas 4). Line and grease an 18cm (7in) square cake tin. Cream butter or margarine with caster sugar and lemon rind in a bowl until light and fluffy. Add egg yolks one at a time, beating well after each addition.

2 Fold in flour and mixed spice alternately with yogurt. Stir in dates.

3 In a separate bowl, whisk egg whites until firm peaks form. Fold them into cake mixture, using a large metal spoon.

4 Spoon mixture into prepared tin and level top. Bake for 20-25 minutes or until cooked. Cool on a wire rack. Cut into squares to serve.

Makes 16 squares

Banana Rye Teabread

90g (3oz) butter or margarine, softened
185g (6oz) soft brown sugar
2 eggs, lightly beaten
1/2 tspn bicarbonate of soda
185g (6oz) rye flour
65g (2 1/4 oz) cornflour
pinch salt
1/2 tspn mixed spice
3 ripe bananas, mashed

Carrot and Pecan Loaf

1 Preheat oven to 180°C (350°F/ Gas 4). Line and grease a 23 x 13cm (9 x 5in) loaf tin. Cream butter or margarine and sugar in a mixing bowl until light and creamy. Add eggs one at a time, beating well after each addition. Add a little flour if mixture begins to curdle.

2 Add bicarbonate of soda, flours, salt, spice and bananas; mix well.

3 Spoon mixture into prepared tin and level top. Bake for 35-40 minutes or until a skewer inserted in centre of loaf comes out clean. Invert onto a wire rack to cool. Serve in slices, spread with butter.

Makes 1 loaf

Carrot and Pecan Loaf

2 eggs, lightly beaten

185g (6oz) soft brown sugar

250ml (8fl oz) oil

125g (4oz) wholemeal flour

125g (4oz) plain flour

1/2 tspn bicarbonate of soda

1 tspn mixed spice

250g (8oz) carrot, finely grated

60g (2oz) pecan nuts, chopped

90g (3oz) dried currants

1 Preheat oven to 180°C (350°F/ Gas 4). Line and grease a 23 x 13cm (9 x 5in) loaf tin. Beat the eggs, sugar and oil in a mixing bowl with a hand-held electric mixer until creamy. Sift in the dry ingredients, mix well, then stir in the carrot, nuts and currants.

2 Spoon the mixture into the prepared tin and level the top. Bake for 1¼ hours or until golden brown and cooked through. Invert onto a wire rack to cool. Serve in slices, spread with butter if liked.

Makes 1 loaf

Chocolate Nut Brownies

185g (6oz) pecan nuts
60g (2oz) plain flour, sifted
45g (1½oz) sugar
125ml (4fl oz) golden syrup
90g (3oz) dark chocolate, chopped
45g (1½oz) butter, chopped
2 eggs, lightly beaten
1 tblspn rum
1 tblspn icing sugar
strawberries to decorate, optional

1 Preheat oven to 180°C (350°F/ Gas 4). Grease and line base and sides of a 18cm (7in) square cake tin. Chop pecans finely by hand (a food processor is not suitable). Transfer to a bowl; add flour.

2 Combine sugar and golden syrup in a saucepan. Stir over moderate heat until boiling. Remove from heat, add chocolate and butter and stir until both have melted and mixture is smooth. Add eggs and rum and stir until combined.

3 Add mixture to flour and nuts and stir quickly until combined.

4 Spoon mixture into prepared tin and level top. Bake for 25-30 minutes or until set. Cool in tin for 10 minutes, then invert onto a wire rack to cool completely. Dust with icing sugar, cut into squares and serve, decorated with cut strawberries, if liked.

Makes 12 brownies

Variation

Omit the rum from the mixture. Do not dust with icing sugar but make a simple icing by combining 140g (4½oz) icing sugar, 15g (½oz) butter and 3 drops of peppermint essence in a heatproof bowl. Stir over simmering water until smooth, then drizzle over the top of the cake before cutting it.

Chocolate Nut Brownies

Lemon and Pecan Loaf

185g (6oz) plain flour
90g (3oz) self-raising flour
185g (6oz) butter
250g (8oz) caster sugar
1 tblspn grated lemon rind
60g (2oz) pecan nuts, chopped
3 eggs, lightly beaten
185ml (6fl oz) milk
5 tblspn lemon juice
2 tblspn sugar

1 Preheat oven to 160°C (325°F/ Gas 3). Line and grease a 23 x 13cm (9 x 5in) loaf tin. Sift flours into a bowl, rub in butter, then stir in sugar, lemon rind and pecans.

2 Combine eggs and milk; stir into mixture. Spoon mixture into prepared tin. Bake for 1 hour or until cooked. Invert onto a wire rack.

3 Heat lemon juice and sugar in a small saucepan until sugar has dissolved, spoon over hot loaf and leave until cool.

Makes 1 loaf

Date and Walnut Teabread

90g (3oz) butter, softened
185g (6oz) soft brown sugar
125g (4oz) chopped dates
90g (3oz) walnuts, chopped
250ml (8fl oz) boiling water
220g (7oz) self-raising flour
1 tspn mixed spice
1 tspn ground ginger

1 Preheat oven to 180°C (350°F/ Gas 4). Line and grease a 23 x 13cm (9 x 5in) loaf tin. Combine butter, sugar, dates and walnuts in a large bowl. Add boiling water and stir until butter has melted. Sift in dry ingredients and mix well.

2 Spoon mixture into prepared tin and level top. Bake for about 45 minutes or until cooked. Cool on a wire rack.

Makes 1 loaf

Apple and Apricot Loaf

250g (8oz) dried apricots, chopped

125g (4oz) dried apples, chopped

300ml (10fl oz) freshly squeezed orange juice

1 x 125g (4oz) cooking apple, grated

1 large carrot, grated

1 tspn mixed spice

2 eggs, lightly beaten

185g (6oz) self-raising flour

1 tspn baking powder

1 Preheat oven to 180°C (350°F/ Gas 4). Line and grease a 23 x 13cm (9 x 5in) loaf tin. Place dried fruit and orange juice in a saucepan. Bring to boil. Remove from heat. Cool to room temperature.

2 Stir in remaining ingredients. Spoon into prepared tin and level top.

3 Bake for 1 hour or until cooked when tested with a skewer. Cool on a wire rack.

Makes 1 loaf

Banana and Orange Loaf

45g (1½oz) butter, softened

125g (4oz) caster sugar

3 bananas, mashed

1 egg

250g (8oz) self-raising flour

½ tspn salt

60ml (2fl oz) orange juice

1 Preheat oven to 180°C (350°F/ Gas 4). Line and grease a 23 x 13cm (9 x 5in) loaf tin. Cream butter and sugar in a bowl.

2 Add bananas and egg and mix well. Sift in flour and salt. Add orange juice. Mix well. Spoon mixture into prepared tin and level top. Bake for 1 hour or until cooked when tested with a skewer. Cool on a wire rack.

Makes 1 loaf

Lemon and Pecan Loaf

Mango Loaf

1 x 470g (15oz) can mangoes

3 eggs, beaten

125ml (4fl oz) oil

250g (8oz) plain flour

125g (4oz) sugar

2 tspn bicarbonate of soda

½ tspn salt

1 tspn ground cinnamon

1 tspn vanilla essence

30g (1oz) macadamia nuts or almonds, chopped

45g (1½oz) desiccated coconut

1 Preheat oven to 180°C (350°F/ Gas 4). Line and grease a 23 x 13cm (9 x 5in) loaf tin.

2 Purée mangoes with 2 tablespoons of can juices. Place purée and all remaining ingredients into a bowl. Beat well. Spoon mixture into prepared tin; level top. Bake for 1 hour or until cooked. Cool on a wire rack.

Makes 1 loaf

Pear Teabread

375g (12oz) self-raising flour

½ tspn salt

90g (3oz) caster sugar

155g (5oz) dried pears, soaked overnight, drained and chopped

2 tblspn pistachio nuts, coarsely chopped

1 tspn grated lemon rind

2 eggs

185ml (6fl oz) milk

60g (2oz) butter, melted

1 Preheat oven to 180°C (350°F/ Gas 4). Line and grease a 23 x 13cm (9 x 5in) loaf tin. Sift flour and salt into a bowl. Stir in sugar, pears, pistachios and lemon rind; mix well.

2 Beat eggs with milk. Add flour mixture and melted butter; beat until well mixed. Spoon mixture into prepared tin and level top. Bake for 1 hour or until cooked. Cool on a wire rack.

Makes 1 loaf

CUT-AND-COME-AGAIN CAKES

This chapter is devoted to family favourites: cakes that evoke memories of childhood and lazy Sunday afternoons. Whether your choice is for a rich fruit cake, a tangy lemon and caraway loaf, the goodness of carrot cake or the sheer indulgence of milk chocolate and fudge, these recipes will make you reach for your apron.

Milk Chocolate Fudge Cake

Hazelnuts, chocolate and brandy combine to make this a moist, rich, utterly irresistible cake that needs no topping other than a fine dusting of icing sugar and a scattering of strawberries to conceal the fact that it sinks in the middle as it cools.

125g (4oz) butter
60ml (2fl oz) brandy
200g (6¹/₂oz) milk chocolate, chopped
6 eggs, separated
185g (6oz) caster sugar
155g (5oz) ground hazelnuts
30g (1oz) plain flour
icing sugar for dusting
strawberries for decorating

1 Preheat oven to 160°C (325°F/ Gas 3). Line and grease a 20cm (8in) square cake tin. Combine the butter, brandy and chocolate in a medium saucepan over low heat. Stir constantly until the chocolate has melted and the mixture is smooth. Set aside.

2 In a mixing bowl, beat the egg yolks with half the sugar until thick and creamy. Beat in the melted butter and chocolate mixture, then beat in the hazelnuts and flour.

3 In a separate bowl, whisk the egg whites until soft peaks form. Gradually add the rest of the sugar and beat for 3 minutes more. Fold one-third of the egg whites into the cake mixture to lighten it, then fold in the remaining egg whites until just combined.

4 Spoon the mixture into the prepared tin and level the top. Bake for 55-60 minutes or until a skewer inserted in the centre of the cake comes out clean. Cool in the tin. To serve, dust with icing sugar and decorate with halved strawberries as shown opposite.

Makes 16 squares

Sour Cream Spice Cake

125g (4oz) butter, softened
185g (6oz) light brown sugar
3 eggs, separated
185g (6oz) plain flour
125g (4oz) custard powder
2 tspn baking powder
1 tspn grated nutmeg
1 tspn ground cinnamon
¹/₄ tspn ground cloves
185ml (6fl oz) soured cream
280g (9oz) blackberry jam

Icing

90g (3oz) butter, softened
140g (4¹/₂oz) icing sugar
2 tspn vanilla essence

1 Preheat oven to 180°C (350°F/ Gas 4). Line and grease a 23cm (9in) round cake tin. Using a hand-held electric mixer, cream the butter with the brown sugar until light and fluffy. Add the egg yolks one at a time, beating well after each addition. Beat in the flour, custard powder, baking powder, nutmeg, cinnamon, cloves and soured cream until combined.

2 Fold in stiffly beaten egg whites. Spoon mixture into the prepared tin and level the top. Bake for 1 hour or until a skewer inserted in the centre of the cake comes out clean. Invert onto a wire rack. When cool, cut into 2 layers.

3 Melt the jam in a small saucepan until easily spreadable. Use the jam to sandwich the cake layers together again.

4 Make the icing by beating the butter, icing sugar and vanilla essence together until light and creamy. Spread over the top and sides of the cake.

Serves 8

Lemon Loaf with Caraway Seeds

185g (6oz) butter
125g (4oz) caster sugar
5 tblspn lemon curd
3 eggs
125g (4oz) self-raising flour
1 tspn caraway seeds

1 Preheat oven to 160°C (325°F/ Gas 3). Line and grease a 23 x 13cm (9 x 5in) loaf tin. Cream the butter, sugar and lemon curd in a mixing bowl until light. Add the eggs one at a time, adding one third of the flour after each addition. Finally stir in the caraway seeds and mix well.

2 Spoon the mixture into the prepared tin and level the top. Bake for 1 hour or until a skewer inserted in the centre of the cake comes out clean. Cool in the tin for 5 minutes, then invert onto a wire rack to cool completely.

Makes 1 loaf

Sour Cream Spice Cake, Milk Chocolate Fudge Cake

Pear and Cinnamon Cake

250g (8oz) butter, softened

185g (6oz) soft brown sugar

4 eggs

250g (8oz) self-raising flour

2¹/₂ tblspn ground cinnamon

5 canned pear halves, drained and sliced

3 tblspn sugar

1 Preheat oven to 180°C (350°F/ Gas 4). Line and grease a 23cm (9in) cake tin. Cream butter and sugar in a bowl. Add eggs, one at a time, beating well after each addition. If mixture shows signs of curdling, add a little flour.

2 Sift in flour with 1¹/₂ tablespoons of cinnamon and beat for 2 minutes. Spoon mixture into prepared tin and level surface.

Arrange pear slices decoratively on top.

3 Mix sugar with remaining cinnamon; sprinkle over pears. Bake for 1-1¹/₄ hours or until a skewer inserted in centre of cake comes out clean. Cool on a wire rack.

Serves 8

Berliner Peach Cake

155g (5oz) self-raising flour

155g (5oz) butter, cubed

75g (2¹/₂oz) caster sugar

1 egg, lightly beaten

750g (1¹/₂lb) fresh peaches, rinsed, dried, halved and stoned

1 tblspn ground cinnamon

icing sugar for dusting, optional

1 Preheat oven to 190°C (375°F/ Gas 5). Grease a 25cm (10in) springform cake tin. Sift flour into large bowl. Rub in butter until mixture resembles coarse breadcrumbs. Add caster sugar and egg and mix to a soft dough.

2 Press mixture evenly onto bottom of prepared tin, making it a little higher at sides than in the middle. Arrange peach halves, cut side down, in circles on mixture; sprinkle with cinnamon.

3 Bake for 50 minutes or until pastry shrinks away from sides of tin. Cool in tin. Just before serving, dust with icing sugar if liked.

Serves 8

Pear and Cinnamon Cake

Walnut Syrup Cake

Orange and Sultana Cake

750g (1½lb) sultanas

400ml (14fl oz) boiling water

125ml (4fl oz) freshly squeezed orange juice

3 eggs

1 tblspn grated orange rind

185g (6oz) soft brown sugar

125ml (4fl oz) oil

350g (11oz) self-raising flour

1 Combine sultanas, boiling water and orange juice in a bowl. Cover and set aside for 1 hour.

2 Preheat oven to 160°C (325°F/ Gas 3). Line and grease a deep 23cm (9in) square cake tin. Beat eggs, rind and sugar together in a bowl until thick and creamy. Gradually beat in the oil.

3 Scrape mixture into a large bowl and sift in flour. Add sultana mixture and mix to form a light batter.

4 Spoon batter into prepared tin and level top. Bake for 1¼-1½ hours or until cooked. Cool in tin for 10 minutes before inverting on a wire rack to cool completely.

Serves 8-12

Walnut Syrup Cake

185g (6oz) butter

350g (12oz) caster sugar

6 eggs

185g (6oz) plain flour

185g (6oz) ground walnuts

90g (3oz) desiccated coconut

walnuts and thin strips of lemon rind to decorate

Syrup

125g (4oz) caster sugar

125ml (4fl oz) water

1 Make syrup by heating sugar and water gently in a small saucepan. Stir until sugar has dissolved, then bring syrup to the boil. Boil without stirring for 2 minutes, pour into a small bowl and cool to room temperature.

2 Preheat oven to 180°C (350°F/ Gas 4). Line and grease a 23cm (9in) flan tin. Cream butter and sugar. Add eggs one at a time, beating after each addition and adding a little flour if mixture begins to curdle. Fold in remaining flour, walnuts and coconut.

3 Spoon mixture into prepared tin and level top. Bake for 35 minutes or until a skewer inserted in centre of cake comes out clean.

4 Cool cake in tin for 2 minutes, then invert onto a serving plate. Spoon a little of the syrup over the cake, arrange walnuts and lemon rind in centre and spoon over remaining syrup.

Serves 8

Dutch Spice Cake

125g (4oz) butter

280g (9oz) soft brown sugar

4 eggs, beaten

125ml (4fl oz) milk

315g (10oz) plain flour

1 tspn salt

1½ tspn bicarbonate of soda

2 tspn cinnamon

¼ tspn ground cloves

¼ tspn grated nutmeg

1 Preheat oven to 180°C (350°F/ Gas 4). Line and grease an 18cm (7in) round cake tin.

2 Cream butter and sugar. Add remaining ingredients, mix well, then beat for 1-2 minutes.

3 Spoon mixture into prepared tin and level top. Bake for 1 hour or until cooked. Cool on a wire rack.

Serves 6

Chocolate Apple Cake

125g (4oz) self-raising flour

½ tspn bicarbonate of soda

30g (1oz) cocoa powder

90g (3oz) soft brown sugar

2 cooking apples, finely grated

2 eggs, lightly beaten

45g (1½oz) pecan nuts, chopped

125ml (4fl oz) oil

icing sugar for dusting

1 eating apple, sliced, for decoration

1 Preheat oven to 180°C (350°F/ Gas 4). Line and grease a 20cm (8in) deep cake tin. Sift flour, bicarbonate of soda and cocoa into a large bowl. Stir in sugar. Make a well in centre and add apples, eggs, pecans and oil; mix well.

2 Spoon mixture into prepared tin and level top. Bake for 40 minutes or until a skewer inserted in centre of cake comes out clean.

3 Cool on a wire rack. Just before serving, dust with icing sugar and decorate with apple slices.

Serves 8

Carrot and Courgette Cake

2 eggs

185g (6oz) soft brown sugar

5 tblspn soured cream

90g (3oz) courgettes, grated

90g (3oz) carrot, grated

125ml (4fl oz) oil

250g (8oz) self-raising flour

¼ tspn bicarbonate of soda

1 tspn mixed spice

Cream Cheese Icing

125g (4oz) cream cheese

30g (1oz) butter, softened

1 tspn vanilla essence

220g (7oz) icing sugar

30g (1oz) walnuts, finely chopped, for decoration

1 Preheat oven to 180°C (350°F/ Gas 4). Line and grease a 20cm (8in) deep round cake tin. In a food processor, combine eggs, sugar, soured cream, grated courgettes and carrot. Process to combine. With motor running, gradually add oil.

2 Sift the flour, soda and spice into a large bowl, stir in the courgette mixture and mix well.

3 Spoon mixture into prepared tin and level top. Bake for 45 minutes or until cooked. Cool in tin for 5 minutes, then invert onto a wire rack to cool completely.

4 Make icing by beating cream cheese, butter and vanilla essence in a bowl until smooth. Gradually beat in icing sugar, spread mixture over cake and decorate with chopped walnuts.

Serves 6

Chocolate Apple Cake

Hazelnut Sponge with Lemon Cream

3 eggs

75g (2½oz) caster sugar

75g (2½oz) self-raising flour

125g (4oz) ground hazelnuts

350ml (12fl oz) double cream

125ml (4fl oz) lemon curd, at room temperature

icing sugar for dusting

1 Preheat oven to 180°C (350°F/ Gas 4). Line and grease a 20cm (8in) round cake tin.

2 Using a hand-held electric mixer, beat the eggs with the caster sugar in a bowl until thick and pale. Sift the flour over the mixture; gently fold it in, using a metal spoon.

3 Sprinkle the ground hazelnuts over the mixture; fold in lightly. Spoon the mixture into the prepared tin and level the top. Bake for 35 minutes. Cool in the tin for 5 minutes, then turn out onto a wire rack to cool completely.

4 In a bowl, beat the cream and lemon curd together until thick. Dust the top of the cake with icing sugar and serve with the lemon cream.

Serves 8

Apricot Fruit Ring Cake

Glazed apricots and pecans make a marvellous topping for this rich fruit cake.

185g (6oz) butter, softened

125g (4oz) caster sugar

3 eggs

90g (3oz) plain flour

2 tspn mixed spice

500g (1lb) dried apricots, chopped

125g (4oz) sultanas

250g (8oz) dried currants

250g (0oz) pecan nuts, chopped

Hazelnut Sponge with Lemon Cream

Topping

15-20 dried apricots

90g (3oz) apricot jam

2 tblspn brandy

20 pecan nuts

1 Preheat oven to 150°C (300°F/ Gas 2). Line and grease a 20cm (8in) ring tin. In a large mixing bowl, cream the butter with the caster sugar until light and fluffy.

2 Add the eggs one at a time, beating after each addition. Add a little of the flour if the mixture shows signs of curdling. Stir in the remaining flour and the spice, then add the fruit and pecans. Mix well.

3 Press the mixture firmly into the prepared tin. Bake for 1½ hours or until the cake has slightly shrunk away from the sides of the tin. Cool in the tin.

4 Make the topping. Soak the dried apricots in warm water for 15 minutes; drain and pat dry with kitchen towels. Heat the jam with the brandy in a small saucepan until just below boiling point.

5 Brush the top of the cold cake with half the jam mixture. Arrange the apricots and nuts decoratively over the top of the cake. Brush the remaining jam mixture over the top.

Serves 8

Apricot Fruit Ring Cake

Banana Cake

3 large ripe bananas, mashed

45g (1½oz) walnuts, chopped

185ml (6fl oz) sunflower oil

110g (3½oz) sultanas

75g (2½oz) rolled oats

155g (5oz) wholemeal flour

2 tspn baking powder

60g (2oz) sugar

1 Preheat oven to 180°C (350°F/ Gas 4). Line and grease a 23 x 13cm (9 x 5in) loaf tin. Combine all ingredients in a large bowl. Beat for 1-2 minutes until well mixed. Spoon mixture into prepared tin and level top.

2 Bake for 1 hour or until cooked. Cool in tin for 10 minutes, then invert onto a wire rack to cool completely.

Serves 8

Carrot and Pineapple Cake

125g (4oz) plain flour

60g (2oz) wholemeal flour

1 tspn baking powder

1 tspn bicarbonate of soda

1 tspn ground cinnamon

1 tspn grated nutmeg

½ tspn salt

150ml (5fl oz) oil

2 eggs, lightly beaten

125g (4oz) carrot, grated

½ x 375g (12oz) can crushed pineapple

1 tspn vanilla essence

Cream Cheese Icing

90g (3oz) cream cheese

15g (½oz) butter, softened

1 tspn vanilla essence

280g (9oz) icing sugar, sifted

125g (4oz) pecan nuts, chopped

1 Preheat oven to 180°C (350°F/ Gas 4). Line and grease a 20cm (8in) cake tin.

Banana Cake

2 Combine all dry ingredients in a large mixing bowl. Make a well in the centre. Add oil, eggs, carrot, pineapple and vanilla. Mix well.

3 Spoon mixture into prepared tin and level top. Bake for 35-40 minutes or until cooked. Cool on a wire rack.

4 Make icing. Beat cream cheese, butter and vanilla essence in a bowl until creamy. Gradually add icing sugar, beating until mixture is very smooth. Spread on cooled cake; press pecans into icing.

Serves 8

Spiced Apple Cake

2 cooking apples, peeled and sliced

185ml (6fl oz) water

125g (4oz) butter

185g (6oz) soft brown sugar

2 eggs, lightly beaten

125g (4oz) wholemeal flour

125g (4oz) self-raising white flour

½ tspn bicarbonate of soda

1 tspn mixed spice

30g (1oz) walnuts, chopped

90g (3oz) currants

185ml (6fl oz) double cream, whipped

sifted icing sugar for decoration

1 Preheat oven to 180°C (350°F/ Gas 4). Line and grease a 23cm (9in) round cake tin. Cook apples with water in a saucepan over moderate heat. Purée apples. Cool.

2 Cream butter and sugar in a bowl. Add eggs; beat until combined.

3 Sift half dry ingredients over mixture. Add half the apple purée. Mix lightly, then beat until just combined. Sift in remaining dry ingredients, add remaining apple purée and beat until combined. Stir in walnuts and currants.

4 Spoon mixture into prepared tin and level top. Bake for 40-50 minutes or until cooked. Cool on a wire rack. When cold, split cake in half, fill with cream and dust with icing sugar.

Serves 8

SPECIAL OCCASION CAKES

Cakes have always been part of celebrations, from birthdays to bar mitzvahs. Christmas wouldn't be complete without the traditional iced cake, and who can contemplate Guy Fawkes Night without a square of sticky gingerbread?

Triple Nut Chocolate Sponge Cake

6 eggs, lightly beaten

250g (8oz) caster sugar

155g (5oz) self-raising flour

50g (1³/₄oz) cocoa powder

100g (3¹/₂oz) walnuts, finely chopped

flaked almonds for decoration

Apricot Syrup

250g (8oz) apricot jam

3 tblspn Cointreau

Choc-butter

155g (5oz) butter, softened

2 tblspn brandy

3 tblspn cocoa powder

140g (4¹/₂oz) icing sugar

60g (2oz) Brazil nuts, chopped

Ganache

350ml (12fl oz) double cream

250g (8oz) dark chocolate, chopped

1 Preheat oven to 200°C (400°F/ Gas 6). Line and grease a 23cm (9in) cake tin. Using a hand-held electric mixer, beat the eggs with the sugar in a bowl until light and fluffy (see Kitchen Tip).

2 In a separate bowl, sift the flour and cocoa together. Stir in the chopped walnuts. Gently fold these ingredients into the egg mixture, if necessary using an electric mixer briefly to combine. Spoon the mixture into the prepared tin and level the top. Bake for about 50 minutes or until a skewer inserted in the centre of the cake comes out clean. Cool on a wire rack.

3 Make the apricot syrup by melting the jam in a small saucepan (or in the microwave oven) until dissolved. Press the jam through a sieve into a bowl, stir in the Cointreau, cover and set aside.

4 Make the choc-butter by mixing all the ingredients except the nuts in a bowl. Beat until light and fluffy, then mix in nuts. Set aside.

5 To make the ganache, bring the cream to the boil in a large saucepan, then simmer for about 5 minutes or until reduced by one-quarter. Off the heat, stir in the chopped chocolate until it has dissolved completely and the mixture is well combined. Pour the ganache into a medium bowl, cover and chill for about 1 hour or until thick enough to pipe.

6 To assemble cake, cut sponge into 3 equal layers. Spread 2 of the layers with apricot syrup, then with the choc-butter. Reassemble the cake, spread the top and sides generously with ganache, then pipe the remaining ganache around the rim of the cake as shown in the illustration opposite. Decorate with flaked almonds.

Serves 8-10

Kitchen Tip
It is important to beat the eggs for about 4 minutes to create a light sponge batter.

Triple Nut Chocolate Sponge Cake

Mandarin Orange Cake

Mandarin Orange Cake

4 eggs

185g (6oz) caster sugar

15g (1/2oz) plain flour

45g (11/2oz) self-raising flour

60g (2oz) custard powder

45g (11/2oz) ground almonds

2 tblspn finely grated orange rind

250g (8oz) apricot jam, melted

Filling

3 egg yolks

125g (4oz) caster sugar

3 tblspn cornflour

2 tblspn Cointreau

250ml (8fl oz) evaporated milk

125ml (4fl oz) double cream, whipped

Topping

250ml (8fl oz) double cream, whipped

125g (4oz) drained canned mandarin segments

1 Preheat oven to 180°C (350°F/ Gas 4). Line and grease a deep 20cm (8in) round cake tin. Beat eggs in a large bowl until thick and pale. Gradually add sugar, beating constantly. Beat for 3 minutes more. Mix flours, custard powder, almonds and rind in a separate bowl; add to the eggs and fold in.

2 Spoon mixture into prepared tin and level top. Bake for 30 minutes or until a skewer inserted in centre of cake comes out clean. Cool on a wire rack.

3 Make filling. Combine egg yolks, caster sugar, cornflour and Cointreau in a medium saucepan. Mix well. Gradually stir in evaporated milk, then heat gently, stirring constantly, until mixture boils and thickens. Cool to room temperature; stir in whipped cream.

4 Cut cake into 3 layers. Spread 2 of the layers with apricot jam, then divide filling between them. Reassemble cake and cover top and sides with whipped cream. Decorate with mandarin segments. Refrigerate until ready to serve.

Serves 8

Chocolate Carrot Cake

125g (4oz) self-raising flour

30g (1oz) cocoa powder

1/2 tspn bicarbonate of soda

90g (3oz) soft brown sugar

1 apple, grated

2 eggs, lightly beaten

90g (3oz) walnuts, chopped

125g (4oz) carrot, grated

125ml (4fl oz) oil

2 tblspn freshly squeezed orange juice

60ml (2fl oz) milk

1/2 tspn mixed spice

Citrus Cream Cheese Icing

125g (4oz) cream cheese, softened

30g (1oz) butter, softened

250g (8oz) icing sugar

grated rind and juice of 1/2 lemon

Chocolate Icing and Decoration

60g (2oz) dark chocolate

15g (1/2oz) butter

125g (4oz) walnuts, finely chopped

125g (4oz) strawberries, sliced

1 Preheat oven to 180°C (350°F/ Gas 4). Line and grease a deep 20cm (8in) round cake tin. Sift flour, cocoa and bicarbonate of soda into a large bowl. Add remaining cake ingredients and mix well.

2 Spoon the mixture into the prepared tin and level the top. Bake for 35 minutes or until a skewer inserted in the centre of the cake comes out clean. Cool in tin for 5 minutes, then invert onto a wire rack to cool completely.

3 To make the cream cheese icing, combine all the ingredients in a medium bowl. Beat until smooth and light.

4 Make chocolate icing. Combine dark chocolate and butter in a heatproof bowl. Stir over simmering water until both chocolate and butter have melted and mixture is well mixed.

5 Set aside about 3 tablespoons of citrus cream cheese icing. Spread rest of icing generously over sides of cake, and roll it in nuts to cover (see Kitchen Tips).

6 Spread chocolate icing over top of cake. Set aside for about 30 minutes or until set. Spoon reserved citrus cream cheese icing into a piping bag fitted with a star nozzle. Pipe a rope border around the rim of the top of the cake. Decorate with sliced strawberries.

Serves 12

Kitchen Tips

Soften the cream cheese by heating it for about 30 seconds in the microwave. The easiest way to coat the sides of the cake is to spread the chopped walnuts evenly on a strip of foil. Place one hand, palm down, on top of the cake, and the other palm up, underneath it. Turn the cake onto its side, taking care not to touch the icing, and roll it gently in the nuts until evenly coated.

Chocolate Carrot Cake

Festive Almond Fruit Cake

155g (5oz) dried apricots, cut into quarters
155g (5oz) red glacé cherries, halved
155g (5oz) green glacé cherries, halved
90g (3oz) raisins
185g (6oz) Brazil nuts
60g (2oz) pitted prunes
125g (4oz) walnuts or pecan nuts
125g (4oz) ground almonds
1/2 tspn baking powder
3 eggs
2 tblspn clear honey
2 tspn vanilla essence

1 Preheat oven to 150°C (300°F/ Gas 2). Line and grease two 18 x 7.5cm (7 x 3in) loaf tins. Combine fruit and nuts; stir in almonds and baking powder.

2 In a second bowl, beat eggs until thick and creamy. Beat in honey and vanilla essence. Pour egg mixture into fruit mixture and mix well. Spoon mixture into prepared tins. Bake for 1 1/2 hours. Cool in tins.

Makes 2 loaves

Rich Moist Christmas Cake

1 x 475g (15oz) can crushed pineapple
500g (1lb) mixed dried fruit
250g (8oz) sugar
125g (4oz) butter or margarine
1 tspn mixed spice
1 tspn bicarbonate of soda
125g (4oz) plain flour
125g (4oz) self-raising flour
2 eggs, beaten
2 tblspn brandy

1 Combine the pineapple (with can juices), mixed fruit, sugar and butter or margarine in a saucepan. Bring to the boil over moderate heat. Boil for 3 minutes, remove from heat, stir in spice and bicarbonate of soda. Cool.

2 Preheat oven to 180°C (350°F/ Gas 4). Line and grease a 23cm (9in) square cake tin.

3 Stir flours, eggs and brandy into mixture until well combined. Spoon into prepared tin and level top. Bake for 1 1/2 hours, then lower oven temperature to 150°C (300°F/Gas 2) and bake for 10-15 minutes more or until cooked. Cool on a wire rack.

Makes 1 cake

Bonfire Night Gingerbread

125g (4oz) butter
250ml (8fl oz) golden syrup
90g (3oz) sugar
1 tblspn marmalade
125ml (4fl oz) milk
125g (4oz) self-raising flour
pinch salt
1 tspn ground ginger
1 tspn mixed spice
1/2 tspn bicarbonate of soda
125g (4oz) wholemeal flour
2 eggs, lightly beaten

1 Preheat oven to 160°C (325°F/ Gas 3). Line and grease a 20cm (8in) square cake tin. Combine butter, syrup, sugar, marmalade and milk in a saucepan. Heat, stirring, until sugar has dissolved. Set aside.

2 Sift self-raising flour, salt, ginger and mixed spice into a large bowl. Add bicarbonate of soda and stir in wholemeal flour. Add butter mixture and mix well.

3 Add the beaten eggs and mix well to make a smooth mixture. Spoon into the prepared tin and level the top. Bake for about 1 1/2 hours or until a skewer inserted in the centre of the cake comes out clean. Cool on a wire rack. Cut into squares to serve.

Makes about 16 squares

Festive Almond Fruit Cake

Chocolate Fudge Torte

90g (3oz) butter

155g (5oz) caster sugar

5 eggs, separated

75g (2¹/₂oz) dark chocolate, melted

2 tblspn brandy

90g (3oz) ground almonds

45g (1¹/₂oz) fresh white breadcrumbs

Topping

100g (3¹/₂oz) dark chocolate, chopped

2 tblspn golden syrup

15g (¹/₂oz) butter

1 tblspn single cream

2 tblspn finely chopped almonds

1 Preheat oven to 180°C (350°F/ Gas 4). Line and grease a 23cm (9in) springform cake tin. Cream butter and sugar. Add egg yolks one at a time, beating well after each addition. Beat in melted chocolate and brandy. Fold in ground almonds and breadcrumbs; mix well.

2 In a separate bowl, whisk egg whites until soft peaks form. Fold into chocolate mixture in 2 batches. Spoon mixture into prepared tin and level top. Bake for 30-35 minutes. Cool on a wire rack.

3 To make topping, combine chocolate, syrup, butter and cream in a small saucepan. Heat gently, stirring, until both chocolate and butter have melted and mixture is smooth. Stir in chopped almonds. Spread topping over cooled cake.

Serves 8

Kitchen Tip

Swiss honey and nut chocolate – the type that comes in a triangular bar – is ideal for the topping on this cake. Omit the chopped almonds.

Alternatively, make a fudge icing by heating 125g (4oz) butter, 125g (4oz) soft brown sugar and 3 tblspn milk in a saucepan, stirring until the butter and sugar have melted. Off the heat, beat in about 315g (10oz) icing sugar.

Chocolate Loaf with Berries

185g (6oz) butter

3 tblspn cocoa powder

250ml (8fl oz) hot water

200g (6¹/₂oz) dark chocolate, melted

250g (8oz) caster sugar

90g (3oz) ricotta cheese

90g (3oz) plain flour

125g (4oz) self-raising flour

2 eggs, lightly beaten

Filling

200g (7¹/₂oz) milk chocolate, chopped

2 tblspn single cream

60g (2oz) chopped nuts

Icing

125g (4oz) dark chocolate, chopped

30g (1oz) butter

125g (4oz) raspberries, hulled

250ml (8fl oz) double cream, whipped

1 Preheat oven to 160°C (325°F/ Gas 3). Line and grease a 23 x 13cm (9 x 5in) loaf tin. Combine butter, cocoa, hot water, chocolate and sugar in a saucepan. Stir over moderate heat until ingredients are combined. Transfer to a bowl. Beat in ricotta cheese, flours and eggs until mixture is smooth.

2 Spoon mixture into prepared tin and level top. Bake for 1¹/₄- 1¹/₂ hours or until cooked. Invert loaf onto a wire rack to cool. Cut into 3 equal layers.

3 To make filling melt milk chocolate in a heatproof bowl over simmering water. Remove from heat and stir in cream and nuts. Set aside for a few minutes, then spread mixture over 2 of the layers. Reassemble loaf.

4 Make icing· by melting chocolate with butter in a heatproof bowl. Stir until smooth. Spread over top and sides of loaf and set aside or chill until set. Serve loaf in thin slices, with fresh raspberries and whipped cream.

Serves 8

Chocolate Fudge Torte

Hot Apple Crumble Cake

90g (3oz) butter, softened
220g (7oz) soft brown sugar
60g (2oz) plain flour
60g (2oz) wholemeal flour
1 tspn baking powder
4 tblspn oat bran
1 tspn vanilla essence
2 eggs, lightly beaten
2 large cooking apples, peeled and sliced
2 tspn lemon juice
1 tspn ground cinnamon

1 Preheat oven to 180°C (350°F/ Gas 4). Line and grease an 18cm (7in) round cake tin. Cream butter with 185g (6oz) of brown sugar in a mixing bowl until light and creamy. Sift in flours and baking powder and mix well. Stir in oat bran and vanilla essence alternately with the eggs. Spoon mixture into prepared tin and level top.

2 Arrange apples over cake mixture, pressing them down lightly. Sprinkle with lemon juice. Mix the cinnamon with remaining brown sugar; sprinkle over apples. Bake for 1 hour or until cooked.

Serves 6-8

Cranberry Cake

250g (8oz) butter
315g (10oz) sugar
4 eggs, lightly beaten
250g (8oz) plain flour
1 tblspn ground almonds
juice of 1 lemon
250g (8oz) fresh or thawed frozen cranberries, rinsed
30g (1oz) flaked almonds

1 Preheat oven to 180°C (350°F/ Gas 4). Grease an 18cm (7in) loose-based round cake tin. Cream butter and 250g (8oz) of sugar. Add eggs with 60g (2oz) of flour. Mix well. Beat in remaining flour, one-quarter at a time. Stir in almonds and lemon juice.

Baked Chocolate Marble Cheesecake

2 Pour half the mixture into prepared cake tin. Top with cranberries. Sprinkle with remaining sugar. Spoon rest of cake mixture into tin, taking care not to disturb cranberries. Level top. Sprinkle with flaked almonds. Bake for 1 hour or until cooked. Serve warm.

Serves 6-8

Baked Chocolate Marble Cheesecake

250g (8oz) golden oatmeal biscuits or digestive biscuits, crushed
100g (3½oz) butter, melted
750g (1½lb) cream cheese, softened
250g (8oz) caster sugar
45g (1½oz) plain flour
1 tblspn vanilla essence
3 eggs, lightly beaten
2 tblspn cocoa powder
100g (3½oz) milk chocolate, melted
350ml (12fl oz) double cream, whipped

1 Combine crushed biscuits and melted butter in a bowl. Press over base and sides of a greased 23cm (9in) springform cake tin. Chill until firm.

2 Preheat oven to 180°C (350°F/ Gas 4). Make filling by blending or processing cream cheese, caster sugar, flour, vanilla essence and eggs until smooth. Divide mixture between 2 bowls. Stir cocoa into melted chocolate; add to one of the bowls and mix well.

3 Spoon plain mixture into biscuit crust. Pour chocolate mixture on top. Using a spatula or skewer, gently swirl mixtures to give a marble pattern.

4 Bake cheesecake for 50 minutes. Cool to room temperature. Chill. Just before serving, decorate with whipped cream.

Serves 8

Ricotta and Sultana Cheesecake

Ricotta and Sultana Cheesecake

500g (1lb) ricotta cheese

juice of 1 lemon

1 tblspn vanilla essence

125g (4oz) caster sugar

3 eggs, lightly beaten

1 tspn ground cinnamon

250ml (8fl oz) double cream

185g (6oz) sultanas

icing sugar for dusting

1 Preheat oven to 180°C (350°F/ Gas 4). Line and grease a 20cm (8in) springform cake tin. Blend or process ricotta cheese with lemon juice, vanilla essence and caster sugar until smooth. While motor is running, add eggs and cinnamon; process for 1 minute more.

2 Transfer mixture to a large bowl. Stir in cream, then add sultanas and mix well. Spoon mixture into prepared tin and level top.

3 Bake for 1 hour. Cool cheesecake in tin for 10 minutes, then carefully transfer to a wire rack to cool completely. Dust with icing sugar just before serving.
Serves 6

Chocolate Dessert Cake

6 eggs, separated

185g (6oz) caster sugar

30g (1oz) cocoa powder

200g (6½oz) dark chocolate, melted

icing sugar for dusting

250ml (8fl oz) whipping cream

2 tblspn brandy

1 Preheat oven to 180°C (350°F/ Gas 4). Line and grease a 23cm (9in) springform cake tin.

2 Beat egg yolks with 125g (4oz) caster sugar until light and creamy. Stir in cocoa and melted chocolate; mix well.

3 In a separate bowl, whisk egg whites until soft peaks form. Fold into chocolate mixture.

4 Spoon mixture into prepared tin and level top. Bake for 35 minutes. Cool in tin, then remove and dust with icing sugar. Whip cream with brandy until slightly thickened.

5 Make caramel by heating remaining caster sugar in a small heavy-based saucepan, moving pan around so that sugar browns evenly. Boil without stirring; cook until it is pale gold in colour.

6 Pour caramelised sugar onto greased foil. When set, break up and decorate cake. Serve with brandy cream.
Serves 6

Chocolate Dessert Cake

BREAD, SCONES AND MUFFINS

Some of the most successful sweet treats can be made in the shortest time; scones and muffins take only minutes to prepare and bake, yet are perfect for teatime with homemade bread and butter.

Wholemeal Bran Bread

500g (1lb) wholemeal flour

125g (4oz) plain flour

30g (1oz) skimmed milk powder

1 tspn salt

125g (4oz) natural bran

1/2 tspn sugar

15g (1/2oz) fresh yeast, crumbled

about 350ml (12fl oz) warm water

1 Grease a 23 x 13cm (9 x 5in) loaf tin. Sift flours into a large bowl. Return husks to bowl. Add milk powder, salt and bran. Mix lightly.

2 Make a well in the centre of the dry ingredients. Add sugar, yeast and 60ml (2fl oz) warm water. Cover bowl with clingfilm and a tea towel; set aside in a warm place for 15 minutes or until foamy.

3 Gradually work yeast mixture into flour, adding enough of the remaining warm water to form a pliable dough. Knead on a floured surface for 5 minutes. Place in a greased bowl, cover with clingfilm and stand in a warm place for l hour or until doubled in bulk.

4 Turn dough onto a floured surface; knead until smooth. Form into a loaf shape, place in prepared tin and stand, uncovered, for 30 minutes or until the dough is well risen.

5 Preheat oven to 190°C (375°F/ Gas 5). Bake loaf for 40 minutes. Remove loaf from tin, place it on its side on oven shelf and bake for l0 minutes. Turn loaf and bake for another 10 minutes. Cool on a wire rack.

Makes 1 loaf

Cheesy Wholemeal Parathas

375g (12oz) plain flour

125g (4oz) wholemeal flour

155g (5oz) butter

350ml (12fl oz) water

125g (4oz) mashed potato

125g (4oz) Cheddar cheese, grated

2 tspn curry powder

1 tspn ground cumin

1 Combine flours in a bowl. Rub in 50g (2oz) butter until mixture resembles coarse breadcrumbs. Stir in the water until combined. Turn onto a floured surface and knead for 5 minutes or until smooth. Set dough aside for 5 minutes.

2 Divide dough into 12 portions. Press each portion out to form a circle. Combine potato, cheese, curry and cumin. Divide mixture between the circles, heaping it up in the middle. Bring up sides of each circle to enclose filling, then roll out each circle to a 10cm (4in) paratha.

3 Melt remaining butter in a large frying pan. Fry parathas, 4 at a time, until golden brown all over and cooked; add extra butter if necessary.

Makes 12

Cheesy Wholemeal Parathas

Hazelnut Bread

3 egg whites

125g (4oz) caster sugar

125g (4oz) plain flour

155g (5oz) roasted hazelnuts

1 Preheat oven to 180°C (350°F/ Gas 4). Line and grease a 25 x 7.5cm (10 x 3in) loaf tin. Beat the egg whites in a bowl until soft peaks form. Add sugar, 1 tablespoon at a time, beating well after each addition.

2 Fold in flour and hazelnuts. Spoon mixture into prepared tin and level the top. Bake for 30 minutes or until light golden brown.

3 Turn loaf onto a wire rack to cool. Wrap in foil. Stand overnight.

4 Preheat oven to 140°C (275°F/ Gas 1). Using an electric carving knife or very sharp knife, slice the loaf thinly. Arrange the slices on baking sheets and bake for 45 minutes or until dry and crisp. Store in an airtight container for up to 1 month.

Makes about 48 slices

Damper

Damper was traditionally an unleavened bread, baked in the coals of campfires in Australia and New Zealand. This is a more sophisticated version.

250g (8oz) self-raising flour

325ml (11fl oz) milk

1 tspn dry mustard

1 tblspn sesame seeds

1 Preheat oven to 200°C (400°F/ Gas 6). Grease a baking sheet. Sift flour into a mixing bowl. Stir in enough milk to give a sticky dough. Knead on a lightly floured surface until smooth. Shape to a round.

2 Place dough on prepared baking sheet. Using your fingers, press it out to a thickness of about 3.5cm (1¼in), retaining the round shape. Mark into wedges with a sharp knife, cutting through top 1cm (½in) only of the dough.

3 Mix mustard and sesame seeds in a cup. Sprinkle mixture over dough. Bake for 30 minutes or until base sounds hollow when tapped with fingers. Serve when freshly cooked.

Makes 1 damper

Hazelnut Bread

Date and Apricot Scones

Date and Apricot Scones

250g (8oz) self-raising flour

60g (2oz) natural bran

60g (2oz) butter or margarine

90g (3oz) pitted dates, finely chopped

90g (3oz) no-need-to-soak dried apricots, finely chopped

250ml (8fl oz) milk

1 Preheat oven to 190°C (375°F/ Gas 5). Grease 2 baking sheets. Sift the flour into a mixing bowl, add the bran and mix lightly.

2 Rub in the butter or margarine until the mixture resembles coarse breadcrumbs; stir in the dates and apricots. Stir in enough of the milk to give a soft sticky dough.

3 Turn dough onto a lightly floured surface; knead lightly until smooth. Press out to a thickness of 1cm (¹/₂in) and cut into rounds with a 5cm (2in) cutter.

4 Arrange scones on prepared baking sheets and bake for 15 minutes or until golden brown.

Makes about 12-14

Gruyère Scones

125g (4oz) self-raising flour

¹/₄ tspn cayenne pepper

¹/₂ tspn salt

90g (3oz) butter or margarine

185g (6oz) Gruyère cheese, grated

1 egg, lightly beaten

about 125ml (4fl oz) milk

beaten egg for glazing

1 Preheat oven to 190°C (375°F/ Gas 5). Grease 2-3 baking sheets. Sift the flour, cayenne and salt into a mixing bowl.

2 Rub in the butter or margarine until the mixture resembles coarse breadcrumbs; stir in the cheese. Add the egg, with enough of the milk to give a soft sticky dough.

3 Turn the dough out onto a lightly floured surface; knead lightly until smooth. Press out to a thickness of about 1cm (¹/₂in) and cut into rounds with a 5cm (2in) cutter.

4 Arrange the scones on the prepared baking sheets, glaze with beaten egg and bake for 15 minutes or until golden brown. Serve warm.

Makes about 15

Featherlight Buttermilk Scones

500g (1lb) self-raising flour

2 tblspn caster sugar

60g (2oz) butter or margarine

250ml (8fl oz) buttermilk or soured milk

185ml (6fl oz) water

milk for glazing

1 Preheat oven to 200°C (400°F/ Gas 6). Grease 2-3 baking sheets. Sift flour into a mixing bowl, add sugar and mix lightly.

2 Rub in butter or margarine until mixture resembles coarse breadcrumbs. Make a well in centre of dry ingredients and add combined buttermilk or soured milk and water all at once. Using a knife, mix until ingredients just cling together to form a soft sticky dough.

3 Turn dough onto a lightly floured surface; knead lightly until smooth. Press out to a thickness of 2.5cm (1in) and cut into rounds with a 5cm (2in) cutter.

4 Arrange scones on baking sheets. Glaze with milk and bake for 10-12 minutes or until golden brown.

Makes 15-20

Spring Onion and Bacon Scones

250g (8oz) plain flour

2 tspn baking powder

1 tspn bicarbonate of soda

1/4 tspn salt

60g (2oz) white vegetable fat, chopped

30g (1oz) butter, chopped

4 rashers rindless streaky bacon, grilled and crumbled

2 spring onions, finely chopped

125ml (4fl oz) buttermilk or soured milk

melted butter for glazing

1 Preheat oven to 190°C (375°F/ Gas 5). Grease 2-3 baking sheets. Sift flour, baking powder, bicarbonate of soda and salt into a mixing bowl.

2 Rub in vegetable fat and butter until mixture resembles coarse breadcrumbs. Stir in bacon and spring onions, with enough of buttermilk or soured milk to give a soft sticky dough.

3 Turn dough out onto a lightly floured surface; knead lightly until smooth. Press out to 1cm (½in) thick. Cut into rounds with a 5cm (2in) cutter.

4 Arrange scones on prepared baking sheets, glaze with melted butter and bake for 15 minutes or until golden brown. Serve warm.

Makes 15-20

Wholemeal Date Muffins

Prepare the batter the day before. Cover and store in the refrigerator, then bake for breakfast or afternoon tea.

155g (5oz) plain flour
½ tspn bicarbonate of soda
½ tspn cinnamon
60g (2oz) sugar
45g (1½oz) natural bran
60g (2oz) pitted dates, finely chopped
60ml (2fl oz) oil
1 egg, beaten
185ml (6fl oz) buttermilk or semi-skimmed milk

1 Sift flour, bicarbonate of soda and cinnamon into a mixing bowl. Add sugar, bran and dates; mix lightly.

2 Make a well in centre of dry ingredients. Add oil, egg and buttermilk or semi-skimmed milk; mix to combine. Cover bowl and refrigerate overnight.

3 Preheat oven to 180°C (350°F/ Gas 4). Grease an 8-cup muffin tin. Divide mixture between muffin cups and bake for 20 minutes. Serve hot with butter.

Makes 8

Featherlight Buttermilk Scones

Oat Bran Muffins

90g (3oz) oat bran
125g (4oz) self-raising flour
350ml (12fl oz) evaporated milk
2 egg whites, lightly beaten
60ml (2fl oz) clear honey
3 tblspn oil

1 Preheat oven to 190°C (375°F/ Gas 5). Grease a 12-cup muffin tin. Mix oat bran and flour in a large bowl.

2 Blend or process evaporated milk, egg whites, honey and oil until smooth. Add to flour mixture and stir until just mixed. Divide mixture between muffin cups and bake for 15 minutes or until cooked.

Makes 12

Cheese Muffins

60g (2oz) cracked wheat
315g (10oz) self-raising flour
2 tblspn sugar
185g (6oz) Cheddar cheese, grated
60g (2oz) butter or margarine
1 onion, finely chopped
1 egg, lightly beaten
about 250ml (8fl oz) milk

1 Soak cracked wheat in a bowl with boiling water to cover for 15 minutes. Drain, rinse, drain again and pat dry on paper towels.

2 Preheat oven to 190°C (375°F/ Gas 5). Grease two 12-cup muffin tins. Sift flour into a bowl. Add sugar, cracked wheat and 90g (3oz) of the cheese. Mix lightly.

3 Melt butter in a saucepan, add onion and cook until tender. Cool slightly. Stir in egg and 185ml (6fl oz) of milk. Add to flour mixture, with enough of remaining milk to make a batter with a heavy dropping consistency.

4 Divide mixture between muffin cups. Sprinkle with the remaining cheese and bake for 20 minutes or until golden.

Makes 24

BEST OF THE BISCUIT BARREL

Who can resist freshly baked biscuits? The aroma alone is enough to tempt the most jaded tastebuds. This chapter contains all the old favourites, from chocolate chip cookies to shortbread, plus a selection of savoury biscuits to serve with cheese.

Chocolate Chip Cookies

375g (12oz) self-raising flour

185g (6oz) butter

90g (3oz) soft brown sugar

90g (3oz) chocolate chips or roughly chopped dark chocolate

1 egg, lightly beaten

1 Preheat oven to 180°C (350°F/ Gas 4). Grease 2-3 baking sheets. Sift flour into a mixing bowl. Rub in butter until mixture resembles fine breadcrumbs. Stir in brown sugar and chocolate chips. Stir in egg, with a knife.

2 On a floured surface, knead biscuit dough until smooth. Roll out to 5mm (^{1}/4in) thick. Using a 5cm (2in) cutter, cut into rounds.

3 Arrange on baking sheets and bake for 10 minutes or until golden brown. Cool on wire racks.
Makes about 24

Ginger Biscuits

200g (6^1/2oz) butter

200g (6^1/2oz) sugar

250g (8oz) plain flour

pinch salt

45g (1^1/2oz) blanched almonds, chopped

4 tblspn roughly chopped preserved stem ginger in syrup

1 egg, lightly beaten

1 egg yolk mixed with 1 tblspn water for glazing

1 Preheat oven to 180°C (350°F/ Gas 4). Grease 3-4 baking sheets. Cream butter in a food processor. Add sugar, flour, salt, almonds, ginger and egg. Process to a stiff dough, adding a little of syrup from ginger if necessary. Roll dough into cylinders, wrap in foil and refrigerate or freeze until firm.

2 Cut cylinders into 5mm (^{1}/4in) discs. Place on baking sheets, glaze with egg yolk mixture and bake for 15 minutes or until golden. Cool on wire racks.
Makes about 60

Macaroons

2 egg whites

125g (4oz) sugar

60g (2oz) ground almonds

1 Preheat oven to 160°C (325°F/ Gas 3). Grease 4-5 baking sheets. Beat egg whites in a bowl until soft peaks form. Add sugar 1 tablespoon at a time, beating after each addition. Add ground almonds in the same way.

2 Drop teaspoonfuls of mixture onto prepared baking sheets, leaving at least 2.5cm (1in) between each for spreading.

3 Put baking sheets in oven and immediately reduce temperature to 110°C (225°F/Gas ^{1}/4). Bake for 2 hours, turn heat off and leave macaroons in oven overnight to dry out completely.
Makes about 60

Chocolate Chip Cookies

Chocolate Nut Wreaths

Chocolate Nut Wreaths

200g (6¹/₂oz) dark chocolate, melted

30g (1oz) flaked almonds, roughly chopped

45g (1¹/₂oz) red, green and yellow glacé cherries, chopped

1 Grease a baking sheet and line with nonstick baking paper Using a teaspoon, spoon a little chocolate onto paper in shape of a wreath; repeat with remaining chocolate.

2 Decorate wreaths with chopped almond slivers and chopped glacé cherries as shown. Refrigerate until firm.

Makes 10-12

Chocolate Almond Biscuits

185g (6oz) dark chocolate

2 eggs, lightly beaten

250g (8oz) sugar

125g (4oz) butter, softened

185g (6oz) plain flour

¹/₂ tspn salt

185g (6oz) blanched almonds, roughly chopped

1 Preheat oven to 190°C (375°F/ Gas 5). Grease 3-4 baking sheets. Melt chocolate in a heat-proof bowl set over simmering water. Remove from heat; allow to cool.

2 In a food processor, combine eggs, sugar and butter. Process until smooth. Add chocolate and process until combined. Add flour and salt and process until smooth. Add almonds, and process to incorporate into dough. Remove dough, wrap it in foil and refrigerate for 30 minutes or until firm.

3 Drop rounded teaspoonfuls of dough onto prepared baking sheets, leaving about 5cm (2in) between each. Bake for 12 minutes or until firm. Cool on baking sheets for 5 minutes, then transfer to wire racks to cool completely.

Makes about 36

Ladyfingers

3 eggs, separated

140g (4¹/₂oz) sugar

¹/₂ tspn vanilla essence

60g (2oz) plain flour

30g (1oz) caster sugar

1 Preheat oven to 180°C (350°F/ Gas 4). Grease 2 baking sheets. Beat egg whites until soft peaks form. Gradually add 60g (2oz) of sugar, beating until stiff peaks form. Set aside.

2 In a separate bowl, beat egg yolks with remaining sugar for about 3 minutes or until mixture falls from beaters in a ribbon. Add vanilla essence and blend in flour. Fold in the egg whites.

3 Put mixture into a piping bag fitted with a plain nozzle and pipe narrow 7.5cm (3in) strips onto baking sheets. Sprinkle with caster sugar and bake for 15 minutes or until golden. Cool on baking sheets for 2 minutes before transferring to wire racks to cool.

Makes about 18

Peanut Butter Biscuits

125g (4oz) plain flour

¹/₂ tspn bicarbonate of soda

125g (4oz) margarine

155g (5oz) peanut butter

90g (3oz) light brown sugar

125g (4oz) white sugar

2 egg whites

¹/₂ tspn vanilla essence

1 Preheat oven to 180°C (350°F/ Gas 4). Grease 4 baking sheets. Sift flour and bicarbonate of soda into a mixing bowl. Set aside.

2 In a processor, combine margarine and peanut butter and process until creamy. Add sugars, egg whites and vanilla essence; process until well combined.

3 Add flour mixture and process to a smooth dough. Roll teaspoonfuls of dough into balls, place on baking sheets. Flatten with a floured fork. Bake for 10 minutes or until golden. Cool on wire racks.

Makes about 60

Thin Walnut Crisps

125g (4oz) plain flour, sifted

60g (2oz) sugar

60g (2oz) walnuts, chopped

1/2 tspn salt

125g (4oz) butter, softened

2 tspn vanilla essence

2 eggs, lightly beaten

1 Preheat oven to 180°C (350°F/ Gas 4). Grease 3 baking sheets. Place flour, sugar, walnuts and salt in a bowl. Mix well.

2 Place butter and vanilla in a processor. Process until soft and creamy. Add eggs with a little of flour mixture; process to combine. Add rest of flour mixture and process to a smooth dough.

3 Drop 9 tablespoons of dough onto each baking sheet. Flatten with back of a spoon to make a 7.5cm (3in) circle. Bake for 8-10 minutes until golden with lightly browned edges. Cool on wire racks.

Makes about 24

Coffee Meringues

1 tblspn instant coffee powder

2 tspn boiling water

4 egg whites

250g (8oz) caster sugar

1/4 tspn cream of tartar

1 tspn coffee essence

1 Preheat oven to 110°C (225°F/ Gas 1/4). Line 4 baking sheets with nonstick baking parchment. In a small cup dissolve instant coffee in boiling water. Cool.

2 Beat egg whites until stiff peaks form. Add caster sugar 1 tablespoon at a time, beating well after each addition. Fold in cream of tartar, coffee essence and coffee mixture.

3 Spoon mixture into a piping bag fitted with a star nozzle. Pipe onto baking sheets. Bake for 1 1/2 hours or until lightly coloured and firm. Cool on wire racks.

Makes about 48, depending on size

Golden Shortbread

250g (8oz) butter, softened

90g (3oz) golden granulated sugar

125g (4oz) wholemeal flour

125g (4oz) plain flour

30g (1oz) rice flour

3 tblspn wheatgerm

1 Preheat oven to 160°C (325°F/ Gas 3). Grease a 20cm (8in) fluted flan tin. Cream butter and sugar. Combine dry ingredients.

2 Add dry ingredients to butter mixture in two lots. Mixing to a firm dough. Turn onto a floured surface and knead lightly for 2 minutes or until smooth.

3 Roll out dough to fit tin. Using a fork, prick dough decoratively. Mark dough into 8 slices, do not cut right through. Bake for 30-40 minutes or until golden brown. Cool in tin for 5 minutes then transfer to a wire rack to cool completely.

Makes 1

Golden Shortbread

Chocolate Macadamia Clusters

300g (9¹/₂oz) dark chocolate, chopped

200g (6¹/₂oz) roasted macadamia nuts, chopped

45g (1¹/₂oz) desiccated coconut

1 Line 2 baking sheets with foil. Melt chocolate in a heatproof bowl over a saucepan of simmering water.

2 Add nuts and coconut, stirring to coat thoroughly.

3 Place heaped teaspoonfuls of mixture on the prepared baking sheets. Chill until set.

Makes about 24

Date and Walnut Cookies

50g (2oz) butter, softened

90g (3oz) soft brown sugar

125g (4oz) plain flour

¹/₂ tspn bicarbonate of soda

30g (1oz) walnuts, finely chopped

¹/₂ tspn vanilla essence

30g (1oz) pitted dates, finely chopped

30g (1oz) walnuts, halved, for decoration

1 Preheat oven to 180°C (350°F/ Gas 4). Grease 2-3 baking sheets. Cream butter and sugar together in a bowl. Add remaining ingredients and mix well.

2 Drop teaspoonfuls of mixture onto prepared baking sheets, allowing room for spreading. Press a walnut half into each biscuit.

3 Bake for 12-15 minutes or until golden. Cool on wire racks.

Makes about 30

Chocolate Viennese Shortbread Biscuits

250g (8oz) butter, softened

60g (2oz) caster sugar

¹/₂ tspn vanilla essence

2 tblspn cocoa powder

185g (6oz) plain flour

45g (1¹/₂oz) cornflour

150g (5oz) milk chocolate, melted

icing sugar for dusting

1 Preheat oven to 180°C (350°F/ Gas 4). Grease 2-3 baking sheets. Cream butter and sugar until light and fluffy. Add vanilla and cocoa and beat until well combined. Sift in flour and cornflour. Mix well. Spoon into a piping bag fitted with a large fluted nozzle.

2 Pipe mixture into shapes on baking sheets. Bake for 12-15 minutes; cool on baking sheets.

3 Dip ends of each biscuit into melted chocolate. Set aside to set. Dust with icing sugar.

Makes about 24

Walnut Crunchies

125g (4oz) butter

155g (5oz) soft brown sugar

2 tblspn golden syrup

90g (3oz) desiccated coconut

185g (6oz) self-raising flour

1 egg, lightly beaten

125g (4oz) walnuts, halved

1 Preheat oven to 140°C (275°F/ Gas 1). Grease 2 baking sheets. Melt butter, sugar and golden syrup in a saucepan over moderate heat. Off heat, stir in coconut, flour and egg. Mix well.

2 Roll teaspoonfuls of mixture into balls. Place on baking sheets, allowing plenty of room for spreading. Press a walnut half onto each biscuit; flatten biscuits slightly. Bake for 20-30 minutes or until golden. Cool on wire racks.

Makes about 18

Chocolate Macadamia Clusters

Cashew Nut Cookies

125g (4oz) butter, softened
75g (2¹/₂oz) caster sugar
1 tspn vanilla essence
1 egg yolk
125g (4oz) plain flour
60g (2oz) self-raising flour
2 tblspn wheatgerm
60g (2oz) unsalted cashew nuts, roasted

1 Cream butter with sugar in a bowl until light and fluffy. Add vanilla essence and egg yolk and mix well. Sift in flours, add wheatgerm and mix to a firm dough.

2 Roll dough into a sausage shape, wrap in foil and refrigerate or chill until firm.

3 Preheat oven to 180°C (350°F/ Gas 4). Grease 4-5 baking sheets. Cut dough into 5mm (¹/₄in) slices, arrange on prepared baking sheets, press a cashew into each and bake for 10-12 minutes until pale gold in colour. Cool on wire racks.

Makes about 48

Apricot Oat Bars

155g (5oz) margarine
250g (8oz) soft brown sugar
220g (7oz) plain flour
1 tspn bicarbonate of soda
155g (5oz) rolled oats
250g (8oz) apricot jam

1 Preheat oven to 180°C (350°F/ Gas 4). Grease a 23cm (9in) square cake tin. Cream margarine and sugar. Beat in flour and bicarbonate of soda. Stir in oats.

2 Press half mixture into tin, spread with jam and sprinkle with remaining mixture.

3 Bake for 30 minutes or until golden. Cool in tin for 10 minutes; mark into bars. Mixture will firm up as it cools. When firm enough to hold its shape, transfer bars to a wire rack to cool.

Makes 18

Sesame Cheese and Chive Biscuits

125g (4oz) self-raising flour

125g (4oz) butter

60g (2oz) blue cheese, crumbled

2 tblspn grated Parmesan cheese

2 chives, snipped

75g (2¹/₂oz) sesame seeds

1 Sift flour into a bowl. Add butter, blue cheese, Parmesan and chives. Mix lightly with fingertips until ingredients cling together and are well combined. Wrap in foil. Chill for 30 minutes.

2 Preheat oven to 180°C (350°F/ Gas 4). Grease 3 baking sheets. Roll heaped teaspoonfuls of mixture into balls. Roll each ball in sesame seeds.

3 Place balls on baking sheets, allowing room for spreading. Press each one down lightly with a fork. Bake for 10 minutes or until light golden brown. Cool on wire racks.

Makes about 20

Pistachio Oat Bran Biscuits

75g (2¹/₂oz) margarine

155g (5oz) sugar

1 tspn vanilla essence

¹/₂ tspn bicarbonate of soda

¹/₂ tspn cream of tartar

125g (4oz) plain flour

45g (1¹/₂oz) oat bran

5 tblspn buttermilk or skimmed milk

30g (1oz) pistachio nuts, chopped

1 Preheat oven to 200°C (400°F/ Gas 6). Grease 3 baking sheets. Cream margarine and sugar. Add vanilla, bicarbonate of soda and cream of tartar. Mix well.

2 Combine flour and oat bran. Add to creamed mixture in three batches, alternately with buttermilk or skimmed milk. Mix well after each addition. Fold in pistachios.

3 Roll teaspoonfuls of dough into balls, place on baking sheets and flatten with a floured fork.

4 Bake biscuits for 10 minutes or until golden. Cool on baking sheets for 2 minutes, then transfer to wire racks to cool completely.

Makes about 30

Oatmeal Biscuits

2 ripe bananas

90g (3oz) soft brown sugar

2 tspn vanilla essence

3 egg whites

125g (4oz) plain flour

125g (4oz) self-raising flour

155g (5oz) quick-cooking oats

¹/₂ tspn bicarbonate of soda

125ml (4fl oz) evaporated milk

60g (2oz) hazelnuts, chopped

1 Preheat oven to 180°C (350°F/ Gas 4). Grease 3-4 baking sheets. Mash the bananas with a fork, or process them in a food processor; transfer to a mixing bowl. Add the sugar, vanilla essence and egg whites. Mix well.

2 Combine the flours, oats and bicarbonate of soda in a separate bowl. Add to the banana mixture alternately with the evaporated milk, beating well after each addition. Stir in the hazelnuts.

3 Drop teaspoonfuls of the mixture onto the prepared baking sheets, allowing room for spreading. Bake for 10 minutes or until the biscuits are lightly browned at the edges. Cool on wire racks.

Makes about 40

Sesame Cheese and Chive Biscuits

Savoury Hazelnut Biscuits

155g (5oz) plain flour
1/4 tspn salt
75g (2 1/2oz) butter, cubed
1 egg yolk

Topping

1 egg yolk beaten with 1 tspn water
1 tblspn sea salt
1 tblspn ground cinnamon
60g (2oz) ground hazelnuts

1 Combine flour and salt in a mixing bowl. Rub in butter until mixture resembles coarse breadcrumbs. Add egg yolk and enough iced water to form a firm dough. Knead lightly on a floured surface. Shape into a flat round and wrap in foil. Refrigerate for 1 hour.

2 Preheat oven to 180°C (350°F/ Gas 4). Grease 4-5 baking sheets. On a lightly floured surface roll out dough to 2.5mm (1/8in) thick. Using a floured cutter, cut out 4cm (1 1/2in) rounds.

3 Arrange on baking sheets. Brush with egg yolk mixture. Combine salt, cinnamon and hazelnuts. Sprinkle over biscuits. Bake for 15 minutes or until golden. Cool on wire racks.

Makes about 48

Parmesan Herb Biscuits

125g (4oz) plain flour
125g (4oz) butter
155g (5oz) grated Parmesan cheese
1 tspn dried oregano
1 tspn dried basil
1/2 tspn Worcestershire sauce
about 3 tblspn dry white wine

1 In a food processor combine flour, butter, Parmesan, oregano and basil. Process until mixture resembles coarse breadcrumbs. With motor running, add Worcestershire sauce with enough white wine to form a smooth dough.

2 On a lightly floured surface, shape dough to a roll about 4cm (1 1/2in) in diameter. Wrap in foil and refrigerate or freeze until firm.

3 Preheat oven to 200°C (400°F/ Gas 6). Cut roll into 5mm (1/4in) slices. Arrange on a greased baking sheet, 1cm (1/2in) apart. Bake for about 12 minutes or until golden brown. Cool on wire racks.

Makes about 48

Sesame Cheese Batons

280g (9oz) plain flour
155g (5oz) Cheddar cheese, grated
250g (8oz) butter, cubed
1 tspn salt
1/2 tspn mild paprika
1 egg beaten with 1 tspn water for glazing
155g (5oz) sesame seeds

1 In a food processor, combine flour, cheese, butter, salt and paprika. Process to a stiff dough. Wrap in foil. Refrigerate for 1 hour.

2 Preheat oven to 180°C (350°F/ Gas 4). On a floured surface, pinch off small pieces of dough; shape into pencil-thin batons about 15cm (6in) in length.

3 Brush with egg mixture. Roll in sesame seeds. Place on ungreased baking sheets. Bake for 15 minutes or until golden. Cool on wire racks.

Makes about 100

Almond Cheese Biscuits

90g (3oz) plain flour
60g (2oz) finely ground almonds
1/2 tspn baking powder
1/4 tspn salt
1/4 tspn cayenne pepper
125g (4oz) butter
60g (2oz) Cheddar cheese, grated
60g (2oz) grated Parmesan cheese
1 egg, beaten

1 Place flour, ground almonds, baking powder, salt, cayenne and butter in a food processor. Process until mixture resembles coarse breadcrumbs. Add cheeses with half the egg. Process to a stiff dough.

2 On a lightly floured surface, shape dough to a long roll about 3.5cm (1 1/4in) in diameter. Wrap in foil and refrigerate or freeze until firm.

3 Preheat oven to 180°C (350°F/ Gas 4). Cut roll into thin slices. Arrange slices on ungreased baking sheets. Glaze with remaining egg. Bake for about 18 minutes or until biscuits are starting to brown around edges. Cool on baking sheets for 2 minutes, then transfer biscuits to wire racks to cool completely.

Makes about 36

Cheese Biscuits

125g (4oz) self-raising flour
1/4 tspn cayenne pepper
1/2 tspn salt
90g (3oz) butter, cubed
185g (6oz) mature Cheddar cheese, grated
1 egg, lightly beaten
up to 125ml (4fl oz) milk

1 Preheat oven to 240°C (475°F/ Gas 8). Grease 4 baking sheets. Combine flour, cayenne and salt in a mixing bowl. Rub in butter until mixture resembles coarse breadcrumbs.

2 Mix in cheese and egg with a knife, adding enough of milk to form a firm dough.

3 On a lightly floured surface roll out dough to 1cm (1/2in) thick. Cut into 5 x 4cm (2 x 1 1/2in) bars. Place on baking sheets and bake until golden brown,.

4 When cool enough to handle, split biscuits lengthwise. Arrange cut-side up on baking sheets and dry out in a 120°C (250°F/Gas 1/2) oven until golden brown.

Makes about 36

USEFUL INFORMATION

Length

Centimetres	Inches	Centimetres	Inches
0.5 (5mm)	$1/4$	18	7
1	$1/2$	20	8
2	$3/4$	23	9
2.5	1	25	10
4	$1^1/2$	30	12
5	2	35	14
6	$2^1/2$	40	16
7.5	3	45	18
10	4	50	20
15	6	NB: 1cm = 10 mm	

Metric/Imperial Conversion Chart

Mass (Weight)
(Approximate conversions for cookery purposes)

Metric	Imperial	Metric	Imperial
15g	$1/2$oz	315g	10oz
30g	1oz	350g	11oz
60g	2oz	375g	12oz ($3/4$lb)
90g	3oz	410g	13oz
125g	4oz ($1/4$lb)	440g	14oz
155g	5oz	470g	15oz
185g	6oz	500g (0.5kg)	16oz (1lb)
220g	7oz	750g	24oz ($1^1/2$lb)
250g	8oz ($1/2$lb)	1000g (1kg)	32oz (2lb)
280g	9oz	1500 (1.5kg)	3lb

Metric Spoon Sizes

$1/4$ teaspoon = 1.25ml

$1/2$ teaspoon = 2.5ml

1 teaspoon = 5ml

1 tablespoon =15ml

Liquids

Metric	Imperial
30ml	1fl oz
60 ml	2fl oz
90ml	3fl oz
125ml	4fl oz
155ml	5fl oz ($1/4$pt)
185ml	6fl oz
250ml	8fl oz
500ml	16fl oz
600ml	20fl oz (1pt)
750ml	$1^1/4$pt
1 litre	$1^3/4$pt
1.2 litres	2pt
1.5 litres	$2^1/2$pt
1.8 litres	3pt
2 litres	$3^1/2$pt
2.5 litres	4pt

Index

Editorial Coordination: Merehurst Limited
Cookery Editor: Jenni Fleetwood
Editorial Assistant: Sheridan Packer
Production Manager: Sheridan Carter
Layout and Finished Art: Stephen Joseph
Cover Photography: David Gill
Cover Design: Maggie Aldred
Cover Home Economist: Annie Nichols
Cover Stylist: Hilary Guy
Published by J.B. Fairfax Press Pty Limited
80-82 McLachlan Avenue
Rushcutters Bay 2011
A.C.N. 003 738 430

Formatted by J.B. Fairfax Press Pty Limited
Printed by Toppan Printing Co, Singapore

JBFP 295 A/UK
Includes Index
ISBN 1 86343 116 0 (set)
ISBN 1 86343 134 9

Distribution and Sales Enquiries
Australia: J.B. Fairfax Press Pty Limited
Ph: (02) 361 6366 Fax: (02) 360 6262
United Kingdom: J.B. Fairfax Press Limited
Ph (0933) 402330 Fax (0933) 402234